Hungary

Károly Szelényi

Hungary

Text by István Lázár and András Székely

Fine Arts Publishing House, Budapest

The authors and the publisher wish to express their thanks to ÉVA KOVÁCS, MIKLÓS MOJZER and ISTVÁN ÉRI for their valuable expert advice.

The photographs were taken with a HASSELBLAD camera using AGFACHROME film.

Translated by TÜNDE VAJDA

Revised by CHRISTINA MOLINARI

Design by GYÖRGY SZEDLÁK

© KÁROLY SZELÉNYI, 1986

ISBN 963 336 405–1

I began my career as a photographer about twenty years ago by photographing museum objects and architectural monuments. From the mid-1970s onwards, I would leave Budapest or my second home in Balatonszőlős from time to time and tour the country, taking photographs of all the interesting areas, sceneries, and buildings that came my way and caught my attention. My first photo album was published in 1978 under the title Balaton and its Environs with Dezső Keresztury's poems. Encouraged by its success, I published another album, Tokaj—Countryside in Changing Light, with text by István Lázár.

In my approach to photographing various parts of the country, I have received much help from my ethnographer and art historian friends, but no less valuable has been the guidance extended by enthusiastic local patriots who love their towns or villages like their own children. I was driven by their great enthusiasm, and went on to translate experiences I had in different parts of Hungary into photographs.

When photographing open country or an object, my first and foremost concern is the co-existence and interaction of man and his environment. More important than making portraits for me is how I discover and provide a way for others to see man in his carefully cultivated vineyard harmonizing succinctly with the countryside, or in front of a peasant cottage that bears the unmistakable signet of its builder. In the course of my wanderings I have very often been captivated by roadside crosses: they express the spirit of community, of human fate. Similarly the master's soul, the character of the man who commissioned the work is very much present in the murals in village churches, the porches of peasant homes, the sumptuous rooms in stately homes.

The pictures in this volume were selected from some two thousand photographs. If the reader does not find the usual pictures here he will perhaps be compensated by others that reveal hidden beauties and a view of Hungary like no other he has ever seen.

Károly Szelényi

If we could tour Hungary by going back in time and begin in Buda—the western half of the capital on the Danube—we would find it difficult to decide where to begin? Should we start half a million years ago? At that time primitive man inhabited the limestone caves under the hill where the Castle overlooks the city today. He already knew how to use fire, and used pebbles from the Danube broken into sharp splinters as tools. The excavation of his occipital bone and petrified footprints near the village of Vértesszőlős, 50 km west of Budapest, in 1965 created an archaeological sensation: for a time he was considered the earliest European.

Eighteen hundred years ago we would have been standing in Aquincum which was the seat of the Roman province of Pannonia. There we might have seen a Roman lady —perhaps the proconsul's daughter, the wife of a legionnaire, or a hetaera—playing dreamily on the water organ, trying to forget that she had been banished to the fringe of the empire, and secretly harbouring Christian sympathies.

Fifteen hundred years ago Attila the Hun, "the Scourge of God", ordered his ornate tent to be set up here on the hill which hid the walls of the smaller amphitheatre in Aquincum. And some eleven hundred years ago the Magyars—who were a pagan race and similar to the Huns both in appearance and character—reached the ancient fords of the Danube way below the place where the river changes its direction for the Balkan Peninsula. The Magyars waded or swam over to the western shore on their inflated sheepskin bags; leading their horses by the rein they saw Pannonia—present-day Transdanubia—for the first time. They settled in the land—the only nomadic Eastern people who were able to found a state in Europe.

About five hundred years ago in Buda King Matthias Corvinus built Renaissance palaces where he invited humanist thinkers and artists from Italy, and sent Italian illuminators' workshops endless orders to supply manuscripts for his Bibliotheca Corviniana. Then, from the mid-16th until the late 17th century, Turkish flags with their half-moon insignia flew from the tower tops; a muezzin prayed to Allah in one church while the spahis used another for a stable. And about fifty years ago, the straggling forces commanded by SS General Pfeffer–Wildenbruch in their retreat from the Red Army climbed through the limestone caverns far below Castle Hill.

The photographer has used Buda as his point of departure, but the frame of reference cannot be anything but the present. His camera is capable of both unflinching sincerity and charming tales. But it would be wrong to believe that a photograph only reveals what is here today, since the present consists of everything that came before it. Luckily, the photographer can move about and work in greater time spans, because the buildings, our material environment and, for that matter, the landscape itself only partially pertain to the present and recent past. They also consist of what has been created and left to us by bygone centuries and our ancestors. At places intact, elsewhere credibly reconstructible, the legacy of millennia is also the setting in which we move and act. Scanning the country with his camera, the photographer shows how strongly the world of modern Hungary is rooted in the past.

North of Buda we have to turn left as the Danube changes its direction. Before arriving at the bend of the river, however, we get two entirely different views. On the western bank we see Szentendre: with its Mediterranean charm it has become a home and workshop for many artists. Serbs fleeing from Turks advancing across the Balkans settled here. They brought with them the Eastern rite of Christianity, and built several churches with magnificent iconostases. The attraction of the town proved strong enough to draw many painters there. If we turn toward the eastern shore, we face Vác, an episcopal see where ecclesiastical architecture was inspired by the Roman Catholic tradition. The Danube has always been a divide between the two rites; it was only for a short time and over a limited area that Eastern Christianity exerted any influence on the western bank.

The Magyars of Chieftain Árpád, who conquered the Carpathian Basin in the Ninth Century and began grazing their animals on its rich meadows, ploughing its fertile lands and fishing in its waters, turned to either Byzantium or Rome when they wished to abandon their pagan beliefs in search of a new faith. As a matter of fact both crosses were extended to them under the guises of welcome and coercion. At around the turn of the millennium Stephen, the first Hungarian king, made a crucial decision: the Magyars were to take up the Catholic faith, thus opening the way for their integration in Christian Europe. Stephen's only son Emeric died an early death; both were later canonised for the historic decision to convert to Catholicism.

North and northwest of today's capital we reach the towns of Esztergom and Visegrád and thereupon a whole new region. This part of the country was one of the centres of Hungarian statehood for centuries. Buda, impoverished heir to Aquincum, did not become the capital city for the tribal confederacy led by the conqueror Árpád; it was neither the capital of the princedom ruled by Géza in the tenth century, nor of the kingdom established by his son, Stephen. King Stephen the Saint and his successors ruled Hungary from the twin centres of Székesfehérvár and Esztergom. Székesfehérvár —once known as Alba Regia—was protected by marches; kings were crowned and buried here. Esztergom, present-day centre of the Catholic Church in Hungary, and the area in its immediate vicinity including Dömös and later Visegrád, was also a centre where royal power was administered. Here the mountains of Börzsöny and Pilis offered military protection as well as forests rich in game.

Today this region is an outdoor museum where some effort is made to preserve natural and historic landmarks, although its aesthetic integrity has fallen victim to the "weekend revolution"—to neatly parcelled tracts of land and villa-building zeal. More recently, a giant power-plant which was designed to broaden the margin of the river into a lake has left its indelible concrete imprint on the ancient scenery.

West of the Danube we tread on Pannonian soil. Many believe that the more than two thousand year-old border of the Roman empire, the *limes,* which here practically corresponded to the natural boundary formed by the Danube, divides the Carpathian Basin to this day in more than merely the geographical sense. People living in its lesser half near the Alps are said to be different from those living in the greater half enclosed in the arc of the Carpathian Mountains. The rolling country is today known as Transdanubia. This part of the world must surely be different from Barbaricum although it would be difficult to say precisely why. The first thing we note about it is that it resembles the Mediterranean as we move farther south. This land is the legacy of Celtic wine-growers and contains many relics from its Roman occupants—villas, dams, aqueducts, stone-paved highways and numbered milestones. This mixture of cultures and times is enhanced by the old altars built here by Middle Eastern pagan cults and some early evidence of the incipient Christian faith as well. We can also trace the development of bourgeois culture and values if we examine architectural styles.

Joseph Haydn lived and worked in Fertőd in the service of the Princes Esterházy, and Ludwig von Beethoven spent time visiting the Brunszvik family in Martonvásár —both villages are in Transdanubia. Incidentally, both chateaus where the composers stayed survived the ravages of war and now house two famous agricultural research institutes.

True, in Transdanubia the rhythm of speech and pace of life are different, the lure of utopias less powerful, caution and scepticism greater: the mentality of "rendering unto Caesar the things which are Caesar's" has always been stronger; the influence of Protestantism was weaker here, and the Baroque Counter-Reformation was more successful. Still I do not subscribe to the idea that regional differences between the various groups of people inhabiting the Carpathian Basin can be traced back to Roman times. Could any similarity to the Transdanubian region be found along the *limes* in Germania, Britannia, Illyria or Dacia? Historical events in recent centuries and relations with different states, different traditions and varying degrees of historical isolation and exposure help to explain our dissimilarities from East and West.

Ingrained customs and stereotypes have also influenced the character of life here. Rolling country is gentle and persuasive, the *puszta* evokes the wild galloping of horses and the mountains the sombreness of cliffs, forests and severe winters. Pannonia has many different regions, each with tranquil countryside and small rivers, and opens up to the sun with self-devotion like a woman. Towns in Pannonia are anything but sprawling: care was taken not to occupy valuable arable land made from forest clearings. These towns are not makeshift winter settlements built by people born and brought up in the *puszta*. They are comfortable and intimate, with the promise of permanence. Foreigners who come here to visit need never feel estranged if they do not speak the local language, since travellers are more than eagerly greeted in their own language by the good folk who live there.

Driving out of Buda to the south or southeast for about an hour we come to a lake. What the appealing waters do not reveal is that the great lake is dying. Geologists—who usually measure life-spans in hundreds of thousands or millions of years—assign the agony of aged Lake Balaton to the mere lifetime of a generation. But the notion of Lake Balaton as a dying lake is absurd to anyone who sees life on its shores: even in winter, many people still go skating, ice-sailing and ice-sledging on its sparkling frozen surface; autumn and spring find the area covered with flocks of birds of passage, and in high season the camping-sites, hotels, and villas are invaded by tourists—sometimes by half a million visitors at a time. No, the lake is very much alive, and according to measurements taken both by professional geological instruments and people who swim there, it still contains some of the purest water in Europe.

But even if we disregard this dire ecological prognosis there can be no doubt that actual dangers, especially those caused by accelerated changes in the flora and fauna of the water, have converted geologists' objective findings into a plea to save the lake. Although the age of Lake Balaton can be measured in hundreds of thousands of years, within recent decades the shoreline has receded, the composition of the water has deteriorated, and valuable species of fish have dwindled: geological old age has set in. Various water and shoreline protection methods may serve to preempt and even reverse this process, and the lake may eventually return to a healthier state as what was vital to it is restored. In the vicinity of Keszthely, there used to be a marshy area called Little Balaton which filtered the waters flowing into the lake. Agriculture benefited little when the marsh was drained, but great harm was done to the lake. Recently, efforts have been made to make this natural filter work again. Hungary is a landlocked country, and the lake has served also as a surrogate sea. What would have happened to the solemn basalt cones, the stone "organ-pipes" rising from extinct volcanos, the Pannonian vineyards and the wine-press houses with their arcades—in fact to the whole delightful character of the land—if this silvery lake had disappeared from the centre.

It is primarily in summer that the Balaton provides an enchanting sporting and recreational area for hundreds of thousands of tourists. Visitors from colder climates may come to take a dip in it during the off-season, but the height of the tourist season proper is during summer. When cold weather fronts bring heavy rains during these months, the mansions, museums and inns offer an attractive alternative to tourists. Also, the geothermal gradient is much lower in Hungary than the European average: instead of the usual 30 to 33 metres, the temperature of the earth crust increases by one centigrade at every twenty metres. Deep-drilling for ores, oil and natural gas often yields hot waters full of dissolved minerals. At other places the hot medicinal springs gush forth freely onto the surface, and their therapeutic effect was recognized thousands of years ago.

One way to develop Balaton would be to exploit the hot and medicinal springs in the immediate vicinity or a bit farther in Western and Southern Transdanubia. The existence of these springs also corroborates the fact that this region was once the site of volcanic activity. Political upheavals, warm friendship and hospitality, paprika, strong wines, the various "fiery" brandies, and the temperature of medicinal springs have insured that the volatile character of this land survives to the present day.

In Transdanubia, even the climate is milder. Blossoming begins earlier in spring than elsewhere in the country, and even if summer is at times more rainy, autumns are often long and mild. Those travelling to countries where the real sun is, in the Mediterranean, stop over on their way around the year.

Crossing the Danube at Mohács in the south we see that the country has an open and vulnerable border in the Carpathian Basin. No wonder that the Ottoman armies eager to conquer Europe crossed the Balkans in early spring. By summer they reached Belgrade and in July or August they fought their battles in Hungary, besieging her castles. They would not have reached Vienna until late in the year, if at all. What, then was responsible for defending Vienna and, with it, Western Europe from the Turkish threat? Were these countries preserved because of Hungary's role as a buffer state? Or did this have something to do with the action radius of the Ottoman army determined by the changing of the seasons? Standing on the battlefield near Mohács, where the Hungarian army suffered a decisive defeat on 29 August, 1526, one cannot attribute the halting of the Turkish troops to action radiuses. For the Turks were still in full power when they reached Hungary, and got tired and demoralised by the time they reached the Austrian border.

Sand, mud and silt were deposited in the southern channel of the vast bay in the Carpathian Basin by the Danube and its tributaries, and until the late 19th century this alluvial plain was impassable because of flooding several times a year. Those compelled to travel then could only make their way through fords and a string of sandy shoals.

There was, naturally, also an abundance of ploughlands and orchards. Yet for centuries cattle-breeders on the Great Plain were well known for the semi-nomadic way in which they worked: the animals were kept in the open, and at most in sheds sheltered from the winds in winter. Large herds of grey Hungarian cattle were driven on foot to faraway markets in Italy, Germany and Austria for centuries. One of the biggest customers was Milan. Although the Turks established a centre of power throughout Hungary except for the border regions which remained under Hungarian—or rather Austrian—rule, the herds continued to be driven to the western markets. Once economic ties are established, they usually prevail through historic changes. One of the main routes for slaughter cattle still leads from the Great Hungarian Plain to the Po valley.

In the region between the Danube and the Tisza, the villages and towns are markedly different from their Pannonian counterparts. Long ago, hundreds of small villages with adobe houses shared the water-washed lands here. What was destroyed by floods could easily be replaced by clay in ample supply. The majority of settlements disappeared in the Middle Ages. The inhabitants moved into market towns which proved less vulnerable to the ravages of war, villeinage, and other hindrances. Later on, when crops began to be worked with more intensive agricultural methods and the waters were regulated by channels and dams, the people moved to outlying, scattered farmsteads and small manors, but kept their town residence for the winter. The fact that farmsteads were joined by roads which were scarce and in bad condition, there was no electricity and hardships prevailed, presented a long-standing problem for the society, which was as difficult to eliminate as poverty. But farmsteads have since proved viable. Their inhabitants often suffer from social rather than economic poverty. By now a number of these farmsteads have disappeared, but the better ones are small and valuable agricultural bases on the Great Plain.

For a long time many believed that the architecture in this region was much more primitive than that in Transdanubia or the border regions because of the unfavourable geographical and historical circumstances. Lately, however, archaeologists have unearthed Romanesque and Gothic remains here.

And the community on the Great Plain, which for centuries kept up contacts with the world market, sometimes even driving animals to market on foot, developed its own cultural centres which were more often influenced by Protestantism than Catholicism. Debrecen has been dubbed "Calvinist Rome". And peacetime, which lasted as long as the period from the 1848 revolution to the First World War, together with the modest agrarian boom around the turn of the century, have combined to produce colourful public buildings in the style of National Romanticism and Art Nouveau: the result was a brief architectural renascence.

People who come to Hungary to see the puszta, the horseherds, mirages and the bleating flocks of sheep may sometimes feel like they are on a reservation. Many old species of animals have survived on the puszta and people wear folk costumes like fancy dress. Yet, while travelling to this protected area, the living museum of Hungarian past, one cannot help noticing how Hungarian agriculture has been transformed. The double character of agriculture is striking: on one hand you can see huge sectors of land belonging to state farms and co-operatives where mechanized, large-scale farming is carried on, and on the other, the private orchards and vegetable gardens on mini-plots with foil tents in which early vegetables are grown. Those seeking the traditional peasant walking along the fields can no longer find him. Most people in the provinces live in families where several occupations are carried on by family members at the same time —the father commutes to town and works in industry, the wife stays at home and works the land, the son works in a trade and the daughter is a white-collar worker. This way all advantages that the various sectors of the economy can offer are enjoyed by the family.

Travelling north we reach a region which is straight out of a fairy-tale. Novelist Gyula Krúdy wrote his short stories and novels on the knights of the fog from this part of the country. I have often crossed the Nyírség at night, and have seen for myself that Krúdy's figures were not imaginary ones. The way mist streaks and fog banks roll out of steaming lands and swim at eye-level above the roads does indeed evoke a world of witches and fairies. Here we find water-mills, ancient churches with murals by local masters, churchyards with totem-like grave-posts, the wealth of apple-trees with roots binding all sand, and above them hosts fleeing in the fog—ladies, mistresses, gallant knights, wandering scholars, the fictitious heroes of light love affairs, gruesome trials, and tragedies.

But we can also choose to believe the contemporary writer, Antal Végh, who was born in this region. He depicts a land ruled by poverty and backwardness, where a greater number of people lead commuter lifestyles than anywhere in the whole country: in search of work men travel everywhere to be guest-workers in their own country— much like southerners in Italy who seek employment in the industrial regions in the North.

Both pictures are true to life—the juxtaposition is necessary not to reveal the contradictions but to see the situation completely. And by the time Antal Végh had written his works on his birthplace, this region too started to develop and take its share of prosperity. True, it is no longer easy to sell the treasure of Szabolcs-Szatmár County —apples. But fruit-growers keep on learning how to get the most out of the lean sandy soil and to produce goods that are more in demand. And they are learning a whole series of new occupations in the factories. Many abandon their commuter lifestyles and either settle in the town where they work or return home where, out of the money they made elsewhere, they build their homes.

Going farther east I reach my own homeland. One can cross the Tisza westwards by ferry, or on the wooden bridge at Cigánd which is drawn offshore every winter and launched again in spring. Travelling in the region between the Tisza and the Bodrog, we come across the Zemplén and Tokaj-Hegyalja mountains: higher up we see deep green forests, and below the vineyards that yield that "sovereign among wines, the wine of sovereigns", and as we look even farther down, the string of villages along the Bodrog.

In actual fact, Tokaj-Hegyalja can thank the Turks for its fame, although even before the Turks had made forays into the region but did not actually take control of it this land had enjoyed a certain popularity. Patak, today's Sárospatak, was for a long time a residence of Hungarian queens. But the wine grown in Tokaj-Hegyalja became a hot item only after Szerémség, now in Yugoslavia, had fallen into Turkish hands, cutting off the availability of wines from Fruska Gora, the Fruit Hills. The wine made in this region is called Tokay everywhere around the world, but it is not grown solely in and around Tokaj itself. From Szerencs to Sátoraljaújhely one good wine after another is produced, the best coming from the vineyards facing east and south below the forests in Tállya, Mád, Tarcal, Erdőbénye, Tolcsva and Sárospatak. Where the very best is made changes from year to year and depends mainly on the weather as well as the vine-stock, the soil and exposure to the sun. Various regions suffer from the annual problems presented by rain, frost and hailstorms. And finally, a lot depends on the cellarmaster's skills: how he attends to the whole process where the grape-juice becomes wine, which part of the several-kilometre-long tunnel cellars he puts the must in, and what kind of barrels he uses. True Tokay wine is as rare as some vanishing species of birds and plants or as ancient murals which emerge from beneath layers of plaster put there in later centuries.

If we go west or southwest we travel on the "Obsidian Road". Man in the New Stone Age carried treasure from the Zemplén Mountains along this route—the black volcanic glass out of which he made his best tools: chisels, sharp knives, the tiny cogs of his corn-harvesting sickle, and the scraper which he flailed the wild beasts with and the domestic animals he killed. The motorway follows this ancient route up to Aszód and Pest, where the Obsidian Road merges with the Shell Road from the south. The two were joined along the Danube by a junction to the Amber Road from the Baltic, which winds up in the Carpathian Basin where today the Austrian–Hungarian–Czechoslovakian borders converge.

The range of hills which seem like mountains to those who live in Hungary extends from the east to the Bükk, Mátra, Cserhát and Börzsöny and even towers over the Danube as the Buda and Pilis Hills. These actually determined the zigzagged border of Turkish-occupied Hungary. Special attention must be called to this demarcation, because in Turkish times for more than 150 years Hungarian life was banished outside these borders to what is today Transylvania in Romania and Upper Hungary in Slovakia. Both were scenes of a great many events in Hungarian history and to this day are the sites of historical landmarks and relics. We can only understand why the development of towns along the present-day borders—Sátoraljaújhely, Ózd, Salgótarján, Balassagyarmat and others—has been periodically disrupted if we consider the historical events affecting the Hungarian borders. Towns have spheres of influence. Eger and Miskolc were not affected by the shifting of the borders, and have managed to retain theirs. The buildings and intellectual values in these towns have been enhanced by having borrowed elements from the area around them, and these towns in turn influence the material and intellectual values in the surrounding area. It is not nostalgia but sober realistic consideration that calls for an explanation of the troubles northern Hungarian towns have encountered. However, after decades of isolation, today economic, cultural and private exchanges along these borders testify to the fact that the borders again foster unity rather than division, and it is not only their immediate vicinity that profits from this but also the neighbouring countries.

Although most people enjoy a higher level of health than ever before, we are concerned about the state of Lake Balaton and our forests. Hungary has also been the victim of acid rain that causes great damage to deciduous and evergreen forests. And we are also worried about indiscriminate exploitation of treasures hidden in the earth. Deep below the surface lie huge deposits of coal which must be conserved. If exploited at all, they should be used in the chemical industry, rather than depleted by power plants.

After having begun in Buda we are now in Pest. We must decide where we have arrived during the long course of its history. A couple of centuries A. D. the small fort Contra-Aquincum defended the ford on the Danube to the land of the Sarmatians where Elizabeth Bridge spans the river today. Eleven hundred years ago Chieftain Árpád led the Magyars here and gave the ruined fort to Muslim Ismaelites. Five hundred years ago the gentry gathered on the field of Rákos and declared Matthias Corvinus King of Hungary—he later acquired the epithet "The Just". Three hundred years ago one could hardly hear Hungarian spoken on the streets of the town, slowly recovering from the Turkish occupation and looking more like a village than one of the world's great capitals. In 1873 Buda, Pest and Óbuda were officially united, and as other settlements began to be linked the city began to take on its modern character. Or we may choose to arrive here in early 1945: all the bridges connecting the twin cities were blown up by the retreating German army, with Pest already liberated and the last fights being fought for Buda.

Arriving in Pest today via Motorway 3, we make a round in Heroes' Square, and remember the great men of Hungarian history. But how much of the original world has remained intact since we started our tour through the country's history? How many times in the course of digging foundations for new houses have bulldozers hit upon Roman remains? How many trees have been felled, and how much of the world hidden under the earth has been disrupted by concrete foundations where a stalactite cave has been sacrificed to build a new multi-story housing unit?

We have finally arrived in Pest. Representatives are preparing for a morning session in Parliament. An inaugural address is being given today at the Hungarian Academy of Sciences, while the stone lions guarding Chain Bridge are being washed, and conference rooms in the hotels along the Danube are packed with businessmen or scientists. Tonight concerts are being given on Margaret Island and the Municipal Assembly Rooms of the Vigadó; tired animals are settling down for the night in the Zoo, and hundreds of young people are dancing folk dances in the new Sports Hall. A political debate is going on in the headquarters of the Patriotic People's Front on Belgrád Quay where a statesman is answering timely questions.

We are at home—and we welcome our guests, with whom we share Budapest, Hungary, Europe and the Earth.

István Lázár

BUDA

Buda is the capital of the kings of Hungary. It is built on quite a high cliff and extends from north to south along its entire length. On the south side, not far from the town, is the citadel, which is excellently provided with all manners of fortifications; moreover, its splendid buildings, with their artistic vaulting and gilded and painted wooden panelling, are magnificient enough to provoke admiration.

Miklós Oláh: Hungaria (1536)

1 View of hotels on the Pest embankment
2 Roof-tiles on the Matthias Church
3 King Matthias Corvinus (1458–1490).
  Copy of a relief in Bautzen (1486)
4 Trinity Square with Matthias Church

2

3   4

"Count István Széchenyi first came up with the idea to join Buda to Pest by means of a Chain Bridge... Designed by the British engineer William Thierney Clark and executed by his deputy, engineer Adam Clark, the bridge was built in ten years and was formally opened to the public on 21 November 1849."
Inscription on the Buda side of the first permanent bridge over the Danube

5

5 Chain Bridge and the former Royal Palace from the Pest embankment
6 The west wing of the Royal Palace now houses the National Széchényi Library

6

[King Matthias]…engaged Italian painters, sculptors, graphic artists, relief-makers, wood-carvers, goldsmiths, stone-masons and architects, paying them handsome sums. Religious services became more glorious as singers were brought from France and Germany to sing in the royal chapel. Even kitchen and fruit-gardeners were invited from Italy, and accomplished farmers who made cheese the Italian, Sicilian and French ways were asked to share their skills. They were accompanied by clowns and actors—whom the Queen especially fancied—along with flutists, trumpeters, violinists and harpists. […] Matthias liked and supported them heartily. He strove to make Hungary a second Italy.

Antonio Bonfini:
Rerum Ungaricum Decades
(1487–1502)

7 Bastion on the west side of Buda Castle, with Lajos Perti's Hussars Monument

8 A good example of Hungarian architecture from the time when Hungary's first millennium of statehood was being commemorated (1896): the neo-Romanesque Fishermen's Bastion with the statue of King Stephen I by Alajos Stróbl

9 The Red Hedgehog House was an inn in the 18th century where actors also occasionally performed

10 Houses in the Castle District have been reconstructed several times—most recently in Baroque and Classicist Revival style—masking Romanesque and Gothic doorways and windows

11 Near the former Buda Town Hall, the new information centre on Trinity Square has been designed to fit in with the architectural environment

9

10

12 The main square in Óbuda: a historic land-mark area where odd-shaped cobblestone streets, courtyards lined by oleanders and geraniums, and small pubs bring back the old days that have been immortalized in novelist Gyula Krúdy's works

13 One of the oldest parts of town, as testified to by its name, Óbuda (Old Buda). It was a Celtic settlement, then a Roman camp with richly decorated villas. One of the most important art treasures which have survived from Pannonia is a floor mosaic depicting the story of Heracles.

The city of Buda is well known to Italians, Germans and Poles, and at the present time also to Turkish merchants, who all swarm there since it is the chief market in Hungary. From whatever direction you contemplate the city and citadel you will find the prospect extremely pleasant; first of all, its situation is so attractive, and, secondly, the buildings and towers in it are so tall and lovely, that you can both admire the beauty of the situation and imagine that you are looking not at buildings made of solid materials but at a magnificent painting. If, on the other hand, you look down from the city on the beautiful countryside spread below you, you will be completely captivated; thus both on this side and on that your eyes are feasted and refreshed.

Miklós Oláh: Hungaria (1536)

THE
DANUBE BEND

On the bottom step that from the wharf descends
I sat, and watched a melon-rind float by.
I hardly heard, wrapped in my destined ends,
To surface chat the silent depth reply.
As if it flowed from my own heart in spate,
Wise was the Danube, turbulent and great.

Attila József: "By the Danube" (1936)
Translated by Vernon Watkins

14 Gate to the Danube Bend: the town of Szentendre was established on the foothills of the Pilis and the Danube. The road to Visegrád and Esztergom, which goes through this little town, is distinguished by many points of historical interest.

15 The Pilis Park Forest in winter

16 Szentendre, with churches and religious artifacts made by followers of Eastern Christianity, has inspired many painters in this century

17 The house of novelist Zsigmond Móricz, where he wrote many of his novels and articles

Doorways withstand the passing of time. Their carved stone frames and thick wood reinforced by iron mountings prove to be stronger than walls. They are faithful witnesses to a time when people built houses to God. Churches were not only places of worship but town meeting-places as well. How many tender glances must have been exchanged in front of this entrance at a time when there were no cafés or other places of entertainment.

18 Baroque gate ornament at Vác, an episcopal see
19 18th-century door of the Blagovestenska church in Szentendre
20 With tree-lined streets and small houses two storeys high, Esztergom has preserved its small-town atmosphere
21 A tourist spot in Szentendre: the Nostalgia Courtyard

18

19

20

21

22 From a boat-house in Óbuda rowers can get to the southern tip of Szentendre Island at Újpest in no time. Rowing up one branch of the Danube and coming back down the other is a challenge for trained rowers. Szentendre Island with several nearby isles and four villages runs for 35 km between the Börzsöny Mountains and Budapest.

In the far forest the lad heard,
at once he jerked up his head,
with his wide nostrils testing
the air, soft dewlaps pulsing
with veined ears pricked, harkening
alertly to those tones sobbing
as to a hunter's slimy tread,
or hot wisps curling from the bed
of young forest fires, when smoky
high woods start to whimper bluely.

Ferenc Juhász: "The Boy Changed into
a Stag Cries Out at the Gate of Secrets"
(1955)
Translated by Kenneth McRobbie

23–24 The Pilis Park Forest

25 The town of Vác, built in predominantly Baroque style, has many fine monuments from later periods as well. Pavilion on the Danube bank from the turn of the century.

26–27 Two battles were fought near Vác during the 1848–49 Revolution and War of Independence. Alajos Degré's poem is inscribed on an 1868 monument to soldiers who fell in battle.

28 The upper-town parish church on Március 15 Square in Vác, built for the Dominicans in 1699–1755

Ha zsarnok lába nyomja e hazát

Ne csüggedj el! hisz ÖK csak nyugszanak

Széttörni békót. szolgalánczokat

Felkelnek újra ÖK a — hösfiak.

29 The coronation cross of the Hungarian kings, made in the mid-13th century and reworked in the 17th, is in Esztergom Cathedral, site of the largest collection of ecclesiastical treasures in the country

30 Figure of an angel from a tapestry used during Lent (*c.* 1500)

31 Silvergilt chalice of Benedek Suky (*c.* 1450)

32 Figure of a prophet from the upper part of the Matthias Calvary (*c.* 1400)

33 High mass in Esztergom Cathedral. The church was built between 1822 and 1856 in Classicist Revival style, on the site of the former 11th-century St. Adalbert's Church.

29

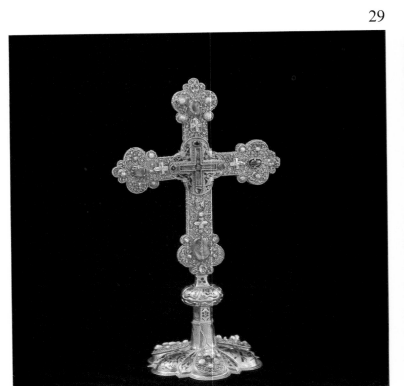

30

31

32

34 The Catholic church in Zebegény was designed by the noted Transylvanian architect Károly Kós in Art Nouveau style inspired by folk art (1909)

35 The "Preacher's Seat" offers the most spectacular view of the Danube Bend

For I have learnt everywhere—and I have seen in every Western nation—that sons carry on the work of their fathers. It may not be the best work, it may not be the most beautifully accomplished or even as perfect as similar things done by other peoples. But it is theirs.

Károly Kós: Old Kalotaszeg (1910–11)

36 13th-century donjon in Visegrád
37 View from the Börzsöny Mountain of Nagymaros and, across the Danube, the Citadel of Visegrád

Apart from the splendid location, this royal palace [in Visegrád] has so many luxurious quarters that it undoubtedly surpasses buildings in other kingdoms. Wherever I visited I have never seen the likes of rooms filled with such lavish decoration.

Miklós Oláh: Hungaria (1536)

NORTHWEST HUNGARY

Depart from me, O cruel Hope!
 Depart and come no more;
For blinded by your power I grope
 Along a bitter shore.
My strength has fail'd, for I am riven
 By all thy doubt and dearth;
My tired spirit longs for heaven,
 My body yearns for earth.
I see the meadows overcome
 With dark consuming blight;
The vocal grove to-day is dumb;
 The sun gives place to night.
I cannot tune this trill o' mine!
 My thoughts are all at sea!
Ah, heart! Ah, hope! Ah, Lilla mine!
 May God remember thee!

Mihály Csokonai Vitéz: "To Hope"
(c. 1803)
Translated by Watson Kirkconnell

38 The Gothic ambulatory in the Benedictine Abbey of Pannonhalma, founded in 966 on St. Martin's Hill

39 One of the most important centres of Hungarian culture in the Middle Ages, the Abbey of Pannonhalma exemplifies how the Benedictines chose the most prominent spots to build their monasteries on. The original monastery underwent considerable changes in the 18th and 19th centuries.

40 The parish church of Sümeg, built in the 1750s, is remarkable for a series of murals depicting the life of Christ. The murals are the chef-d'œuvre of young Franz Anton Maulbertsch, an Austrian painter who received numerous commissions from Hungarian churches.

41 The reliquary of St. Ladislas, king of Hungary (1077–95) is a masterpiece of goldsmithing from the early 1400s, and is preserved in St. Ladislas Chapel of Győr Cathedral

42 Tombstone of Júlia Vajda, immortalised as Lilla in the poems of Mihály Csokonai Vitéz (1773–1805)

43 A four-towered castle was built around the ancient donjon of the Csák clan on Lake Tata under Louis the Great (1342–82). His son-in-law Sigismund, King of Hungary and Holy Roman Emperor, received envoys from East and West here. During the reign of Matthias it was rebuilt in lavish Renaissance style. Today it houses the Domokos Kuny Museum where many splendid archaeological, historical and industrial relics found in the town of Tata and vicinity are exhibited.

44 The Baroque entrance and church tower of the hermitage at Majk, once owned by Camaldulian monks

45 The hermitage consists of 17 separate houses, each built by an aristocratic family for this extraordinary order. Each house, complete with a small chapel, was inhabited by one monk. The closest specimens of this kind of Baroque architecture are in Poland.

46 Csesznek Castle, built around 1300, guarded the mountain passes in the Upper Bakony. During the fight against the Habsburgs in the early 18th century, it was one of the strongholds of the defence waged by Francis Rákóczi and the freedom fighters.

47–48 The palace of the Festetics family in Keszthely was built in the 18th century. One of the many eccentrics in the family, György Festetics (1755–1819) was a generous patron of the arts and took a lively interest in the country's agrarian development. He organized art festivals in the palace and founded an agricultural academy called Georgicon in 1797. Part of it is now open to visitors.

49 Statue of St. John of Nepomuk, patron
saint of boatmen, fishermen and millers,
who watches over bridges and rivers in the
village of Bakonybél

50 Statue of St. George the Dragon-slayer at
Lövő (1711)

51 Pietà at Páli (1690)

52–53 Statues from the chapel of the Lengyel-
Tóti family on St. George's Hill, built in the
second half of the 18th century. Figure from
the altar and St. George the Dragon-slayer
from the façade

50

51

52

53

Episcopal residences built in the 18th century are dominant features in architecture in Western Hungary

54 View from Veszprém Castle. In the fore-
ground, the statues of King Stephen and
Queen Gisela by József Ispánki (1938)
55 The episcopal palace at Győr, seen from
the Danube
56 The episcopal palace at Székesfehérvár,
built on ruins of a basilica from the time of
King Stephen I

57 Main façade of the episcopal palace at Szombathely

58 Sopron on the frontier with Austria earned the nickname "most loyal town" when the inhabitants decided by special plebiscite in 1921 not to secede from Hungary

Not far from the Alps, one can hear German spoken in the streets of Sopron and Kőszeg, both by the inhabitants and tourists passing through. These proud and well-kept small towns guard the noble traditions of bourgeois culture.

59 The Firewatch Tower has become a landmark in Sopron, a town which has escaped the ravages of fire several times

60 Kőszeg Castle was the scene of a famous fight against the Turks. Led by Captain Miklós Jurisics, the Hungarian soldiers defended the town and castle in 1532. The main square is named after the captain, and the tower is called Heroes' Tower to commemorate the feat.

61 Arcaded courtyard in Jurisics Square

62 Italianate arcaded courtyard in Fabricius House at Sopron

63 The pharmacy in Jurisics Square was opened in 1777. Once exhibited in the Budapest Museum of Applied Arts, its furnishings have been returned and the pharmacy opened as a museum.

64 The Lion Pharmacy in Sopron is still in business. The trade-sign depicts the beast the shop was named after: the style is Naïve-Romantic, late 19th century.

*What you don't trust to stone
and decay, shape out of air.
A moment leaning out of time
arrives here and there,*

*guards what time squanders, keeps
the treasure tight in its grasp —
eternity itself, held
between the future and the past.*

*Sándor Weöres: "Eternal Moment" (1938)
Translated by Edwin Morgan*

65 The Széchenyi Mansion in Nagycenk, built
between 1750 and 1840 for the great aristocratic family which gave the country the
great 19th century reformer, Count István
Széchenyi. One wing of the mansion is a
museum.

66 Donjon of the Kinizsi Castle at Nagyvázs-
ony, which has towered above the valley of
the Eger-víz for six centuries. The castle
was once home to King Matthias' famous
commander and fighter against the Turks,
Pál Kinizsi and his wife, Benigna Magyar,
who had elegant taste. Today a museum,
the building was a gaol in the 18th century.

67 One of the finest monasteries built at the turn of the 12th and 13th centuries is the one at Ják. The basilica, with its nave and aisles closed off by arcaded choirs, is filled with sculptured ornaments. This sculptural ornament was partly destroyed: in Turkish times the faces that were easier to reach were maimed by raiding Muslims complying with the Prophet's ban on representing the human form.

68

69

68 Figure of a lion on the northern apse of Ják church
69 A symbolic, decorative representation on the outer wall of the main apse
70 The nave

70

71

Buda is the capital of the kings of Hungary. It is built on quite a high cliff and extends from north to south along its entire length. On the south side, not far from the town, is the citadel, which is excellently provided with all manners of fortifications; moreover, its splendid buildings, with their artistic vaulting and gilded and painted wooden panelling, are magnificient enough to provoke admiration.

Miklós Oláh: Hungaria (1536)

Small churches, far from the thoroughfares of history and the main tendencies of art history research, sometimes exhibit delightful local variations on great historical styles and speak eloquently of their builders. In most cases their construction was disrupted by the Mongol Invasion of 1241–2.

71 The chapel at Pápóc was built in the second half of the 13th century
72 The bevelled archway entrance to the church at Lébény, which belonged to a Benedictine monastery founded in 1208
73 Romanesque church in the village of Csempeszkopács

THE LAKE BALATON DISTRICT

76

77

78

79

[King Matthias] ... engaged Italian painters, sculptors, graphic artists, reliefmakers, wood-carvers, goldsmiths, stonemasons and architects, paying them handsome sums. Religious services became more glorious as singers were brought from France and Germany to sing in the royal chapel. Even kitchen and fruitgardeners were invited from Italy, and accomplished farmers who made cheese the Italian, Sicilian and French ways were asked to share their skills. They were accompanied by clowns and actors—whom the Queen especially fancied—along with flutists, trumpeters, violinists and harpists. [...] Matthias liked and supported them heartily. He strove to make Hungary a second Italy.

Antonio Bonfini:
Rerum Ungaricum Decades (1487–1502)

80 View of the vineyards of Badacsony Hill
   from the house of Róza Szegedi, wife of the
   poet Sándor Kisfaludy
81 The Mill Pond at Tapolca. The pond is fed
   by karstic waters
82 The ridge of Badacsony Hill in winter fog

83 View of Badacsony from the southern shore
84 Szigliget and vicinity

I live among gardens. I too am a garden.
Earth, stones, sun, grapes, moon, wine press
my food. I flower to desire, deepen to valleys.
I am a still cocoon and my bitterness thins
like the clear sweet oil of almonds.

Dezső Keresztury:
Balaton and its environs (1978)

There, death is a dear relative:
a crypt stands as the family grave,
a guardsman, vigilant, steadfast.
A cool wind ruffles its grass-hair —
and its angles and its door
have ivy coats thickly massed.

Sándor Weöres: "Homeward Bound"
(1935)
Translated by Edwin Morgan

85 The medicinal waters of Hévíz
86 The medicinal bath at Hévíz
87 The Romanesque church of Egregy
   near Hévíz

I will take you now again to Balaton,
to the tower above the lake. Kisses
                              afloat on
your face from the wind: from me!
                    Huge, full,
the moon sails over rough Badacsony hill,
its bright watery bridge almost at our feet.
Can you hear the chirping of this holy night?
The soul swings open: it is vigilant,
but still the nerves of space envelop it
and between the infinities above and below
crickets strike up a fortissimo.
zither-twangs of u *and sparks of* i,
rich and thick, u-ru-kru *and* kri-kri,
ringing out loudly and ringing round
like rings of foam that encircle an island,
richer and richer, as they did last year
                    and before
and always will: weave it into your soul,
weave yourself into its warp and weft and
you will become a sigh, and understand.

From the cycle "Cricket Music" (1947)
by Lőrinc Szabó
Translated by Edwin Morgan

88 Porch of a peasant home in Somogy County
89 Thatched house in Balatonszőlős
90 The Calvinist church at Balatonszőlős
91 Peasant dwelling in the Balaton Uplands:
   the wine-cellar

89

90

91

SOUTHWEST
HUNGARY

92 The Hungarian Academy of Sciences guest-house at Pécs
93 Pécs Cathedral, centre of the bishopric founded in 1009. The neo-Romanesque church was rebuilt a hundred years ago. One of the most important collections of Romanesque stone carvings is on display in the crypt.

94 Street in Pécs
95 French painter, Victor Vasarely, the leading name in Op Art, donated a considerable portion of his œuvre to the town of Pécs, where he was born in 1908. The building of the Vasarely Museum.
96 Statue of Nike by Makris Agamemnon in Pécs

97 Today a Catholic church, the mosque of Ghazi Khasim Pasha on Széchenyi Square, Pécs, is the largest architectural monument surviving from the Turkish occupation
98 The Saracen pharmarcy in Pécs, with wall-tiles from the Zsolnay Ceramic Factory

98

97

When I recall my birth-place, I too think of a little house in the country. But I can remember only the house with its two tiny rooms and the earth-floored kitchen in between. The yard stretched as far as the eye could see. When I first struggled over the well-worn threshold, the infinite world lay at my faltering feet.

Gyula Illyés: People of the Puszta (1934)

102

103

101 The fort of Szigetvár was taken by the Turks in 1566
102 Peasant home in the village museum of Sellye in the Ormánság region, a characteristic ethnic island in Baranya County
103 Folk costume in the Sárköz region

THE GREAT PLAIN

We had long left Gyöngyös and Kápolna behind when I began to get into conversation with my fellow travellers. Up to then I had been silent as Szluha in the national assembly. Nor would I have spoken now, but when we emerged on the plains of Heves, the clergyman began to abuse the flat lands, whereupon I deemed it my duty to speak in their defence, and what is more in true Petőfi style, that is to say with appropriate churlishness. I can't help it. Let no one abuse in my hearing my beloved, the French, cream cheese and noodles, and the plains. — From this time onward I had a continuous dispute with the reverend gentleman, who I soon came to realize was primo *a tremendous anti-Hungarian,* secundo *a tremendous aristocrat and* tertio *a tremendous ass. He had no other fine qualities.*

Sándor Petőfi: Traveller's Letters to Frigyes Kerényi (1847)

I've always said that the Great Plain was the most wonderful province in the world, but my great predilection for it has never carried me away so far as to praise its roads, nor, with all solemnity, shall I do so now. To be able to do this I should have to murder my conscience and banish the experiences I've so bitterly acquired. Oh no, I can't do that, with the best will in the world!

And as if a journey on the Alföld were not enough by itself, my trip was preceded by 10, yes ten, days of rain, and on top of that it rained in torrents for two days of the journey. Now you can imagine what a jolly time I had—but no, you can't, not by any means, even if you were to burst with effort. True, my cart had a canvas top, but so much mud clung to the wheels that in the truest sense of the word we were forced to stop every hundred paces and scrape the sticky black buttery stuff off the spokes ... if only the person I'm thinking of would spread it on his bread and choke with it! Don't worry, I've thought of someone who doesn't matter, a bad poet.

Sándor Petőfi: Traveller's Letters to Frigyes Kerényi (1847)

106

107

And once we have identified what characterizes a nation, we must discuss the ethnic quality now artistically valuable—the "spirit" of the building which can hardly be translated, for it so purely belongs to Hungarian architecture—it is so unique to this nation—that it is like nothing else in Hungarian fine arts. It is massive and enduring. Here is the Hungarian imagination at play with mirage.

Lajos Fülep: Hungarian Art (1923)

There was money in the towns on the Great Plain, especially during the economic boom in the last third of the 19th century. (Some said that the Debrecen Council decided to build a theatre just to show they could afford it.) The town centres of Kecskemét, Szeged and Kiskunhalas were built around the turn of the century and were patterned after a special Hungarian version of Art Nouveau introduced by Ödön Lechner

108 The centre of Kiskunfélegyháza

109 The "Fancy Mansion" in Kecskemét. Ornamentation by Géza Márkus

110 House in Szeged built in Art Nouveau style

111 One-time symbol of the puszta: Hungarian
   grey cattle
112 Symbol of modern peasant life: the foil tent

113 15th-century brick castle at Gyula
114 Folk dance festival in Kalocsa
115 Girl in the audience

...There are two Szegeds: one was built by Count Kunó Klebelsberg, the other by Gyula Juhász. One was constructed from ruddy stones, the other from lines of poetry like grey panes. Two cities—one created by a minister, the other by a poet —may yet be trying to outdo each other.

Zoltán Szabó: The Love of Geography (1942)

116 The National memorial park at Ópusztaszer, near Szeged, in the south. The Magyar tribes would hold their meetings to discuss judicial affairs here.
117 The town of Szeged was totally rebuilt after the great flood of 1879

118 The Gothic Franciscan church in Szeged was built in the second half of the 14th century

119 The university of Szeged is named after a student who was expelled: the poet Attila József (1905–1937)

120 Folk belief holds that a stork's nest should
     not be knocked down or those living in the
     house will have bad luck
121 Grazing flock
122 The Tisza at Tápé

Lord, it's very hard to get
your politics, try as we may.
Bad times—you can see it yet.
That world war that came our way,
crisis and such we had to shoulder—
you know it seemed at times we'd rather
snuff it than go on. Made us bolder
in rapping your saints, you too, father.

Imre Csanádi: "Silent Prayer of
Peasants" (1941)
Translated by Edwin Morgan

124

123 A row of cellars in Hajós
124 Windmill near the town of Gyula

125 The Bridge of the Nine Arches at the Hor-
tobágy, the steppe in the east
126 Kitchen from a peasant home at Tiszacsege
127 Porch of a peasant home on the Great
Plain

128 The library of the College at Debrecen
129–130 The neo-Classicist Great Church of
Debrecen, built at the beginning of the 19th
century. The independence of Hungary
from Austrian domination was proclaimed
here in 1849, and the Temporary Diet was
convened in 1945.

128

129   130

THE NYÍRSÉG DISTRICT

134

135

136

137

138

138 Calvinist church in Csenger. Its construction was begun in the 14th century

139 Detail from the Altar of Passion in the Minorite Church of Nyírbátor, executed in 1737 and donated by János Krucsay and his wife

140 Interior of late 15th-century church at Nyírbátor. With its excellent acoustics it is an ideal place for concerts.

141 Wooden tiles are a characteristic building material in the Nyírség district

142–5 Wooden towers are symbols of communal life in tucked-away villages. The silent bell or abandoned wooden tower were symbols in literature during the first half of the 20th century.

142

143

144

145

NORTHERN
HUNGARY

147

146

146 The Castle of Boldogkő, built in the 13th
century
147 On the banks of the Bodrog
148 The Cistercian abbey church of Bélapátfal-
va from the first half of the 13th century
149 The Rákóczi Castle at Sárospatak, viewed
from across the Bodrog

150 School-leaving ceremony in the Rákóczi Secondary School at Sárospatak

151 Chalices and cups in the Calvinist Church collection at Sárospatak

152 This fossil of a fish is ten million years old (private collection)

153 The Library in the Calvinist College at Sárospatak has survived remarkably intact through stormy centuries. It is especially noted for its wealth of 17th-century material

154 Detail of a globe from the scientific collection

151

152

153

154

Depths of forgotten churchyards terribly
consume all that they were, yet might
they not
have now become light dust which longs
to be
dissolved in sky, unable to forget
how thirst for knowledge drove relentlessly?

Perhaps the altitudes admit them all,
and, made delirious with light, they flash
from star
to star, zig-zagging bugs, until they fill
their great rapacious souls. They swallow
there
sugar of light to store when back they fall.

It does not matter. Here their heavy bones
remain so that the turning earth is slowed.
Shoved in forever, all these skeletons
must treat with us the orbit's ancient road
where their coevals buried their remains.

Zoltán Jékely: "In the Startower"
(1936)
Translated by Alan Dixon

155 Romanesque round church at Kissikátor
156 All Saints' Day in the Eastern Orthodox cemetery at Tokaj
157 The presence of a tombstone with Hebrew inscription suggests that a yewish community once flourished in this area
158 Széphalom. Mausoleum of Ferenc Kazinczy, 19th century poet, literary organizer and reformer of the Hungarian language, in the garden of his home

155

156

157

160

161

162

163

164 The Main Square in Eger with the Minorite Church and the statue of István Dobó, 16th century captain of Eger Castle

165 18th-century iconostasis in the Eastern Orthodox church at Eger

166 A Gothic relic in Eger, a town built primarily in the Baroque style

167 Interior of the Cistercian church at Eger

168 Wrought-iron gate in the County Council building by Henrik Fazola (1750s)

169 Door of the 18th-century Franciscan church built on the site of a former Turkish mosque

170 Mural by F. A. Maulbertsch (1793) on the chapel ceiling in the former Lyceum, now a teachers' training college

171 Main façade of the Lyceum in Eger, built between 1763 and 1785 by Jakab Fellner. Behind the history of the Lyceum is a dream that did not come true. Bishop Károly Esterházy intended to found a university in Eger, with law and medical faculties. The Scola Medicinalis opened its doors in 1769 when he was still a bishop. It was supposed to be transferred to another building which was finished under the rule of Joseph II. But he never granted university status to the school.

Before autumn's swift clouds the moon bound to and fro, wishing to see itself reflected in the cool well water before departing—torn away. It holds out like an obstinate woman, but not for long. The corn shucks rattle. After the mad chase, the last hare sits on it haunches, pricks up its ears, and gradually stiffens into sculpture as catastrophe approaches.

Gyula Illyés: "Early Darkness" (1965)
Translated by William Jay Smith

172 Sleighing in Szilvásvárad in the valley of the Szalajka
173 Charcoal burning in the Bükk hill

174 The De la Motte Mansion at Noszvaj, built
in the second half of the 18th century. The
style of Noszvaj Mansion suggests the
serenity of France before the revolution,
although its interior may have been com-
pleted before it was taken over by its
French owner. Ancient gods Zeus, Apollo
and Artemis, in the murals may have been
copied from fashionable engravings.

175 The great hall in Noszvaj Mansion

176 The Turkish Baths in Eger
177 Hot spring in Aranyoskút
178 Medicinal waters at Egerszalók
179 Lean soil, pastures fit only for sheep, and
    endless forests: the Zemplén Mountains

180 Crypt of the church at Feldebrő
181 Fragment of a mural with Byzantine
touches representing Cain in the crypt of
Feldebrő church

182 Sacristy of the Franciscan church at Szé-
csény started in 1332
183 Detail of mural from the Baroque mansion
at Pétervására
184–6 Baroque, Renaissance and Gothic windows at Sárospatak

183

184

185

186

187 Hollókő. The castle and the entire village
     are registered architectural landmarks
188 Thatched peasant home in northern Hun-
     gary

187

189 Town centre of Salgótarján. Today's architecture strives for a new mode of expression more impatiently than that in great periods of the past. Some historians of architecture acknowledge that only the achievements of industrial architecture have absolute value. Indeed, we have very few town centres as consistent and modern as the one in Salgótarján, where the architects were not bound by tradition and had freedom to fashion the centre of a 20th-century industrial town.

190 Thermal plant at Visonta

191 Füzér Castle, built in the 12th century. The Viennese court ordered it to be razed at the end of the 17th century, so that it would not fall into Hungarian rebels' hands.

192 Hegyköz: passage between the valleys of the rivers Bodrog and Hernád. Landscape at Füzérradvány.

PEST

The Danube just flowed on. And playfully
The ripples laughed at me as I reclined,
A child on his prolific mother's knee
Resting, while other thoughts engaged her mind.
They trembled in time's flow and in its wake
As tottering tombstones in a graveyard shake.

Attila József: By the Danube (1936)
Translated by Vernon Watkins

193 The "Gothic House", as novelist Ferenc Herczeg called the Parliament building on the left bank, built in 1885–1904

194 The bulding of the Hungarian Academy of Sciences, with the statue of its founder, Count István Széchenyi

195 Conference hall in the building of the Academy

I don't do this to be cheered for it. Nor because I want to inspire others to do similar deeds. Not everybody could do what I have done. I am a soldier, and unmarried.

Count István Széchenyi's words in 1825, when he offered his annual income to found the Hungarian Academy of Sciences

196 Statues adorning the façade of the Vigadó, the Municipal Assembly Rooms, in Pest
197 Mosaic on the façade of an Art Nouveau house from the turn of the century, evoking the mood of the millenary celebrations. In the swirl of modernism, art history nearly condemned Revivalist styles and the Art Nouveau. Today we prefer to trace the roots of fashionable post-Modern art back to the pre-Modern, and show more understanding of the ideals of the upper middle classes who envisioned their own past

198 The Millenary Monument in Heroes' Square commemorates the thousandth anniversary of the founding of the Hungarian state

199 The Pest embankment

The dicky brickheart misses beats but
                                 never stops,
and if fate should someday strip the
                                  town of stones,
it would rise again in time by the right
                                  it stores.

Its stones and beams and walls are not
                                  what make it,
a hundred demolitions could not break it:
its eternity is redeemed when death
                                  would take it.

Now every light is out; faith dawns
                                  through misty air.
I know this will be put on record,
                                  somehow, somewhere:
I lived here and never wished to live any
                                  place but here.

István Vas: "Budapest Elegy" (1957)
Translated by Edwin Morgan

200 Károlyi Gardens and residence of the president of the 2nd Republic, now the Petőfi Literary Museum

201 The riverside promenade in front of the Forum Hotel. Once considered an old-fashioned pastime, "promenading" is back in style. Old candelabra, grilled dustbins and benches—once considered "street furniture"—are back in style.

TOTÓ LOTTÓ TOTÓ TOTÓ
HOSSZUHETÉNYI NÉPI EGYÜTTES
TANAR:
KASZAS JANOS
ZENE:
HOSSZUHETÉNYI
FÚVÓSZENEKAR
ARTEXSPORTGO
ORION ORION

Oh, for far-off monkeyland,
ripe monkeybread on baobabs,
and the wind strums out monkeytunes
from monkeywindow monkeybars.

Monkeyheroes rise and fight
in monkeyfield and monkeysquare,
and monkeysanatoriums
have monkeypatients crying there.

Sándor Weöres: "Monkeyland" (1955)
Translated by Edwin Morgan

203

204

202 Folk dance festival in the new Sports Hall
203–4 Moments in the Zoo

205 Interior of the Hotel Atrium-Hyatt
206 The Western Railway Station, designed by
the Eiffel firm, Paris, was the terminus of
the Hungary's railway line

207–8 The traditional fireworks on Constitu-
tion Day (20 August)
209 A bird's-eye view of Budapest

1714 1111

© Képzőművészeti Kiadó, Budapest 1986
Printed in Hungary, 1986
by Kossuth Printing House, Budapest